# ANIMAL CROSSING:
## Decorating and Customizing

CHERRY LAKE PUBLISHING • ANN ARBOR, MICHIGAN

# CHERRY LAKE PRESS

Published in the United States of America by Cherry Lake Publishing
Ann Arbor, Michigan
www.cherrylakepublishing.com

Reading Adviser: Beth Walker Gambro, MS, Ed., Reading Consultant, Yorkville, IL

**Cherry Lake Press** is an imprint of Cherry Lake Publishing Group

Library of Congress Cataloging-in-Publication Data has been filed and is available
at catalog.loc.gov

Cherry Lake Publishing Group would like to acknowledge the work of the
Partnership for 21st Century Learning, a Network of Battelle for Kids. Please
visit http://www.batelleforkids.org/networks/p21 for more information.

Printed in the United States of America
Corporate Graphics

# Contents

Chapter 1

# The New You

**A**re you the kind of person who's always looking for a way to put your own spin on things? Do you like to try out new fashions and redecorate your room? *Animal Crossing: New Horizons* might be the game for you. This smash hit for the Nintendo Switch is all about building your own

In *Animal Crossing*, you are completely in charge of your own little town. You'll get to decide how buildings are laid out, how everything is decorated, and more.

You can build the bedroom you wish you had in real life or try out wacky new decorating styles.

**virtual** community on an island paradise. Players get to decorate their own homes, build up a town full of shops, and much more. There is plenty of room for creativity. Almost everything in the game can be customized. Every player gets a unique environment that they can change as often as they like and show off to their friends.

You get to start making design decisions almost as soon as you turn the game on for the first time. One of your first tasks will be to design a character to represent you in the virtual world. Don't worry about making bad decisions. You will be able to change everything except your character's name as often as you like once you start playing.

All player-made characters in *Animal Crossing* have the same height and body shape. When you start the game, you'll be able to choose from eight different skin tones. They are all shades of peach and brown, much like ones people can have in real life. Later on, you can unlock the ability to try out wacky skin

Some players like their *Animal Crossing* characters to look like themselves, while others go for completely new looks.

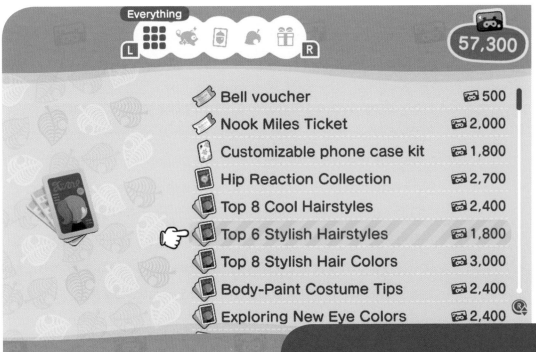

Everything

57,300

| | |
|---|---|
| Bell voucher | 500 |
| Nook Miles Ticket | 2,000 |
| Customizable phone case kit | 1,800 |
| Hip Reaction Collection | 2,700 |
| Top 8 Cool Hairstyles | 2,400 |
| Top 6 Stylish Hairstyles | 1,800 |
| Top 8 Stylish Hair Colors | 3,000 |
| Body-Paint Costume Tips | 2,400 |
| Exploring New Eye Colors | 2,400 |

New hairstyles and other features are added to the game from time to time, so keep an eye on Nook Stop.

colors such as green and purple. You're also limited to just a few styles and colors for your hair at first. If you want to expand your options for hair and skin, you'll need to earn some Nook Miles. Then visit the Nook Stop machine at the Resident Services building in the center of town. Exchange your miles for items with names such as "Top 8 Cool Hairstyles" or "Body-Paint Costume Tips." There are several different ones to buy, and each one will give you new options for customizing your character's looks.

You can also choose a look for your character's face. You can adjust the shape and color of your eyes. There are also a few different noses and mouths to choose from. These options might seem fairly simple. But you might be surprised at how different they can look when you combine them in interesting ways.

The biggest changes in your character's appearance will come from changing clothes. You'll find hundreds of different clothing items as you play. Some are as simple as jeans, sneakers, or sweatshirts in every color of the rainbow. Others are more like wild costumes. Want to dress like a superhero or a pirate? You can do that, and much more. Visit the Able Sisters shop in your town each time you play to see what's in stock. Some items will be on display on the store's shelves. But if you go to the fitting room, you'll have even more options to try. The available fashions change every day, so there are always new things to see.

To change your appearance after starting the game, you'll need to get a mirror for your house. Mirrors can be **crafted** or purchased from Timmy and Tommy at the Nook's Cranny shop. (Their

When using a wardrobe, you can easily mix and match all the different clothes you own.

available stock changes every day. Check back later if they don't have what you're looking for.) There are all kinds of mirror types, and any one will work. Simply place it in your house and use it to access the character creation screen. To change your clothes, you'll need a wardrobe. Craft or buy one, then place it in your house. When you use it, you'll see all of the clothes you have in your **inventory** or home storage. Mix and match to pick out the perfect outfit. You can also change clothes one item at a time by selecting the item in your inventory and choosing to put it on. This is much slower, though. You also won't be able to see how it looks until you wear it. The wardrobe works much better!

Sometimes new clothing and character creation options are added to the game as free updates. They usually go along with different seasonal celebrations. For example, spooky costumes might show up around Halloween. A Santa Claus outfit might show up near Christmas. Keep an eye on the local shops and the town's notice board to keep up with what's new.

Unlike in real life, *Animal Crossing* makes it easy to get back discarded old clothes if you regret it later.

## Whatever You Like

Creativity is a big part of *Animal Crossing*. Don't feel like you have to make your character look a certain way. Some players try to design characters that look like their real-life selves. Others do the exact opposite. Some keep a consistent look for their character, while others make big changes. You can make your character cool and stylish, or just fun and goofy. You can also mix and match however you like. Everyone is free to look the way they want to.

If you play a lot, you might eventually find that you simply have too many clothes. Your home storage and inventory both have limits on how many items they can hold. When this happens, you'll need to sell some of your things back to Timmy and Tommy to make space. If you change your mind and want to get back an old item, simply visit the Nook Stop and choose Nook Shopping. Then choose the clothing catalog. This will show you a list of all the clothing items you have ever owned, even ones you have sold or traded away. It costs Bells to get them back, but you can re-purchase anything. This means you don't have to wait for it to come back in stock at the Able Sisters store.

Chapter 2

# A Happy Home

**W**hen you start playing *Animal Crossing: New Horizons*, your only shelter is a small tent. But if you play enough, you can eventually have a huge house with several rooms. What can you do with all that space? Decorate it and fill it with furniture and other cool objects, just like people do in real life. It's a free space where you can do anything you

At the beginning of the game, your village will look more like a campsite.

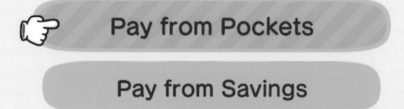

| Loan Balance | **298,000** Bells |
|---|---|
| Savings Balance | **437,175** Bells |

👉 **Pay from Pockets**

**Pay from Savings**

> Housing upgrades start to get expensive very quickly, but you'll make more than enough money to afford it if you play a lot.

like. Want to set up a cozy bedroom? Go ahead. Want to have a spooky room full of giant spiders and skeletons? You can do that too.

Soon after you start the game, a character named Tom Nook will help you upgrade your tent to a simple one-room house. In return, you will owe him 98,000 Bells. This might seem expensive, but you'll soon make plenty of virtual money by doing everyday things in the game. You can repay Tom Nook as quickly or slowly as you like. Once the debt is fully paid, you can start the next upgrade on your house. This will enlarge your main room, and it costs 198,000 Bells. Upgrades continue to follow this pattern, with each one costing more than the last. You always have to pay Tom Nook back before starting the next upgrade.

A fully upgraded house has a large main room and three smaller rooms on the first floor. It also has a basement and a second story with another large room. As your house grows, you will also unlock more

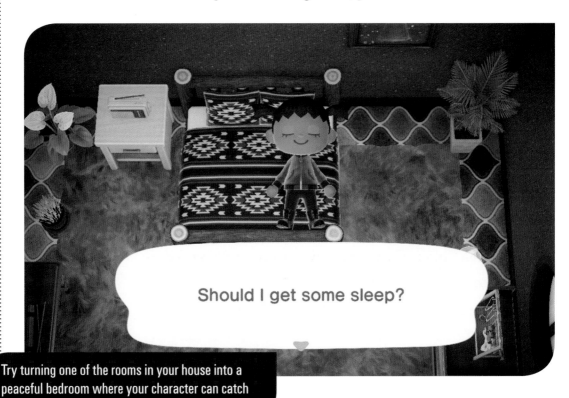

Should I get some sleep?

Try turning one of the rooms in your house into a peaceful bedroom where your character can catch up on some much-needed rest.

Red.

Pink.

Yellow.

Black.

A different color.

**Tom Nook**

**Could you please select a roof color from this list, hm?**

As your house gets bigger, you will unlock more ways to change its exterior looks.

options to customize its **exterior** appearance. For example, you can change the color of your mailbox and roof. To do this, you'll need to talk to Tom Nook and pay a small fee. Customizing the exterior is free once you have fully upgraded your house and paid off all loans. It will take some time to do this, though. The total cost for all the upgrades is several million Bells!

You can change the flooring and wall covering in each room of your house. Flooring and wall coverings are inventory items. To use one, select it in your inventory. Then choose "Place on Wall" or "Place on Floor." The new style will appear in the room you are in.

## Making a Good Impression

From time to time, you will receive letters from the Happy Home Academy. This organization keeps a watchful eye over your home decorations and sends awards when you decorate well. You'll get points for increasing the size of your house. It also helps to make sure each room has a good amount of furniture. Some items also go better together than others. Try to match the same style or color for all the furniture in a room, for example. Furniture should be facing in directions that make sense. For example, you don't want a couch off in the corner and facing a wall. You should also be sure to hang things on the walls. The more you work on your interior design, the better your score will get. The Happy Home Academy will mail you trophies and plaques that you can display to show off your decorating achievements to visitors!

The previous wall or floor will be moved to your inventory. You can only use each one in a single room. So, if you want multiple rooms with the same floor, you will need multiple copies of that floor item.

Furniture and other items are also stored in your inventory. To place a piece of furniture in your house, highlight it in your inventory. Then select the "Place Item" option. Want to move it around? Walk up to the item and hold down the A button. Your character will reach out and grab the item. While holding A, use the

left stick to make your character push or pull. You can
also move the stick toward your character's side to
spin the item and change the way it faces. Some items
can only be placed in certain areas. For example,
large items might need a certain amount of space.
Some decorations can only be hung on walls. Smaller
items can often be set on tables or other surfaces.

There are hundreds of different items you can
use to decorate your home in *Animal Crossing*. Some
can be purchased from the Nook's Cranny store run

All you have to do to move furniture is grab it and
start dragging!

by Timmy and Tommy. Others are rewards for completing various tasks and storylines in the game. Your fellow villagers will give you things from time to time. Sometimes you'll even find items lying around the island. You can also craft your own furniture and decorations once you have some supplies and DIY (do-it-yourself) recipes.

Once you start collecting items, your inventory will fill up quickly. Luckily, your house comes with built-in storage. Press the right arrow button while you are inside to access your home storage. At first, you can store up to 80 items here. Each housing upgrade you purchase will unlock additional slots, up to a total of 800. You'll need all of them if you play a lot!

When you are in your house, try pressing the down arrow button. This will take you to an overhead view where it is easier to arrange your furniture and decorations. Use the left stick to move the cursor around. Press the plus button to switch between the walls and the floor. Use the right stick to move the camera around and look at the room from different angles. Place the cursor over an item and you can move it, rotate it, or send it to your storage with a single button press. This is the fastest and easiest way to tweak your room once you've dropped a few decorations.

Of course, your house is about more than just looks. Many of the items you place can also be used. For example, you can sit in chairs and lie down on beds. Other items do all kinds of different things if you walk up to them and press the A button. A mirror will let you change your appearance. Even small items like toasters and coffee grinders will spring to life when you activate them. Play around and experiment! And if you're having a hard time seeing, press the up arrow button. It lets you switch the lights on or off in each room of your house.

A stereo will let you play different music once you've bought some songs from Nook Stop.

## Chapter 3

# The Great Outdoors

Your house isn't the only place you get to design in *Animal Crossing*. The entire island is your canvas, and you have a lot of freedom to turn it into something truly unique. Naturally, your outdoor options are a little different than indoor decoration.

Much like indoors, you can drop furniture and other items anywhere there is space outside. However, you will not have access to the overhead view where

Leif

Oh! Hello! Isn't this the most perfect day to shop for flowers?

Leif will sell you gardening supplies that you can't get anywhere else. It's always worth seeing what he has for sale.

you can move objects around using a cursor. This means you'll have to use your character to drag and rotate objects around to get them exactly where you want. There are a lot of decorative objects that are meant for outdoor use. For example, you can unlock park benches, vending machines, street lamps, and more. However, you can also feel free to plop down a stereo or a couch in your backyard. There are no rules!

You can also decorate outdoor areas using plants. There are a couple of different ways to plant flowers. First, you can simply buy seeds from Nook's Cranny or a visiting salesman named Leif. Dig a hole with your shovel, then find the seeds in your inventory and plant them. Use your watering can to make sure they get water each day, and they will eventually bloom. If you use your shovel on a flowering plant, you can dig up the whole thing. Then you can dig a hole elsewhere and replant it.

There are eight different kinds of flowers in the game. Each type comes in several different colors. However, it's not easy to find them all. Only certain flowers are **native** to your island, and shops will only sell a limited range of flower types and colors. Native flower **species** vary from island to island, so not all players will start with the same plants. One way to get new ones is to try visiting mystery islands. You can reach these islands by purchasing special tickets using Nook Miles. Sometimes they will have new plants. Other times, you might find the same ones that grow back home. You can also get new plants by visiting your friends' islands. Once there, you can ask to dig up your friends' native flowers or buy seeds from their local shop.

Tired of the same basic flower colors? Try **breeding** new ones. First, you'll need two flower plants of the same species, but different colors. For example, you might plant a red tulip and a yellow tulip. Plant them diagonally from each other. Water both flowers frequently and keep checking them each day. Eventually, a new flower plant should sprout nearby. Depending on the original flowers you planted, the new one could be a unique new color. For example, the red tulip and white tulip in our example will produce an orange tulip. Each flower species has a different set of color combinations that can be bred. If you want a certain color, you might need to go through several steps of breeding. Experiment and see what color combinations you can create!

As long as you are next to a hole, you will have the option to plant saplings or trees from your inventory.

You can plant trees on your island much like flowers. Purchase saplings from shops if you want to grow regular trees. If you want more fruit trees, simply dig a hole and plant a piece of fruit. Each island starts with one type of native fruit. If you want others, you'll need to trade with friends. If you're lucky, your character's mom might also mail a piece of fruit to you. Then you can plant it and grow even more fruit!

Fruit comes in handy if you want to uproot a tree and move it to a new location on the island. Start by eating a piece of fruit. Any kind will work. Then use your shovel on a tree. This will place the entire tree in your inventory. If you try to dig up the tree without eating fruit, your shovel will simply bounce off the trunk.

At the start of the game, your island will have weeds growing all over the place. You can pick them if you want a nice, clean-looking area. They can be used as crafting ingredients or sold to Timmy and Tommy. Weeds will continue to grow all the time. You'll need to pick them frequently if you don't want them to cover your island. If you come back to the game after taking a long break, you might be surprised how many have popped up!

Fences are a great way to section off different parts of your island. For example, maybe you want to make a flower garden that no one will walk on. Or maybe you want to give your villagers their own private yards. Tom Nook will give you your first fence pieces after you've built up your island a little bit. After that, you can craft more or purchase it from Nook Stop with Nook Miles. If you place fence pieces next to each other, they will automatically connect and form corners as needed.

Once you get far enough in the game, you will unlock the Island Designer app for your NookPhone.

## Keeping Score

Want to find out how your island measures up? Talk to Isabelle in the Resident Services building and ask her for an **evaluation**. She will tell you your island's rating from one to five stars. The rating goes up as you grow more plants, add decorations, and invite more villagers to move in. When she tells you the rating, Isabelle will also give you hints to let you know what your island is missing. Keep aiming for better and better evaluations. Reaching the highest star rating is the only way to unlock certain items in the game!

At first, this app will only let you create walking paths on your island. But if you visit the Nook Stop, you can purchase the ability to create raised cliffs or dig out bodies of water. You can also unlock different types of paths. Once you have these, you can shape the land however you like. Raise and lower different areas. Create rivers and lakes. Or turn your entire island into a single flat landscape. It's all up to you!

You can take on larger construction projects on the island by talking to Tom Nook in the Resident Services building. Tom can help you move buildings to new locations. He can also help you build bridges or inclines. These are expensive projects, so be sure to save up plenty of Bells!

Chapter 4

# Design It Yourself

**A**nimal Crossing: New Horizons comes with a huge variety of built-in clothing and furniture designs. But even with so many options available, you might have an idea for something different you'd like to see in the game. Luckily, the game allows you to create your own custom designs from scratch.

To get started, simply open up your NookPhone and select the Custom Designs app. You'll see a few premade designs and a bunch of empty slots. Select

The Custom Designs app gives you the freedom to draw just about anything you can imagine.

a slot, then choose "Change Design." Now you'll see a screen with drawing tools and a blank white square. The blank drawing area has grid lines to help you draw carefully. You can create anything you want in this space. Try drawing a repeating pattern, such as polka dots or stripes. Or you can draw a picture. The tools on the right side of the screen can help you form a variety of shapes. You also have a bunch of different colors to choose from. The only limit is your creativity.

Want to wear your custom design as a shirt or face paint? Simply select it from the Custom Designs app, then choose "Wear." If you want to create designs for other types of clothing, you'll need to visit Nook Stop and purchase the Pro Designs upgrade using Nook Miles. Once you have it, open the Custom Designs app and press the R button. Now you have access to patterns for different shirts, coats, dresses, and hats.

You can also share your designs or check out designs from other players. To do this, check out the computer screen at the back corner of the Able Sisters shop. This is the Custom Design Portal. You can post your creations or search through the many, many items created by other *Animal Crossing* fans.

Your custom designs are good for more than just clothes. If you are indoors, you can use your designs as wall and floor coverings. You can also hang them on the walls as artwork. Simply open the Custom Designs app, choose a design, and decide where to place it. And once you have the Island Designer app, visit the Nook Stop to purchase the custom design path permit. This gives you the ability to lay down your designs as walkway tiles anywhere outdoors!

Certain furniture items and accessories can also display your custom designs. Visit a DIY bench and say that you want to customize something. Then choose an item from your inventory. Along the

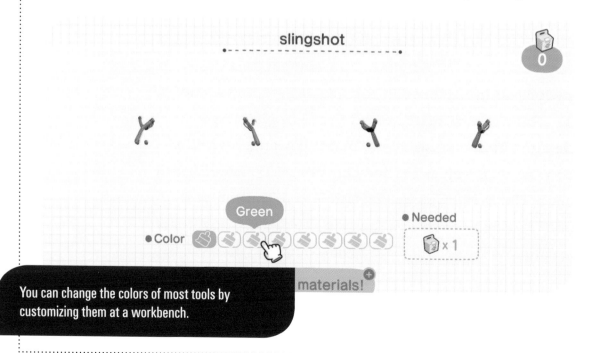

You can change the colors of most tools by customizing them at a workbench.

## Looking For Inspiration

*Animal Crossing* players love to show off their creations. Online, you'll find countless screenshots and videos of other people's fashions, island layouts, and home decor. Looking at these is a great way to get ideas for your own creations. But inspiration can come from anywhere. You might want to redecorate your *Animal Crossing* house after seeing pictures of someone's real-life home. Or maybe you want your character to wear clothing that looks like something your favorite TV character wears. Be creative, and always be willing to try new things. If you don't like something, you can always change it!

bottom of the screen, you'll see options for customizing the item's appearance. Some will let you choose "Custom Design" as an option here. Not all items work with this, so you'll have to try different ones and see what happens.

Talk to Isabelle in the Resident Services building if you want to use one of your custom designs as an official town flag. Once you do this, you'll see the flag flying in the **plaza** and other locations as you play. Isabelle will also let you compose theme music for your island. You don't need advanced music skills to make something that sounds good, so feel free to play around.

There are nearly limitless options for putting a personal touch on your *Animal Crossing* island. Use your imagination, try new things, and don't forget to have fun!

# Glossary

**breeding** (BREE-ding) intentionally mating plants together to produce new plants with certain features

**crafted** (KRAF-tid) made or built something

**evaluation** (ih-val-yoo-AY-shuhn) the process of judging something

**exterior** (eks-TEER-ee-ur) the outside of something

**inventory** (IN-vuhn-toh-ree) a list of the items your character is carrying in a video game

**native** (NAY-tiv) found naturally in a certain place

**plaza** (PLAH-zuh) a public space often located in the central area of a town

**species** (SPEE-sheez) a particular category of animals or other living things

**virtual** (VUR-choo-uhl) existing in a computer program, but not in real life

# Find Out More

## BOOKS

Cunningham, Kevin. *Video Game Designer*. Ann Arbor, MI: Cherry Lake Publishing, 2016.

Loh-Hagan, Virginia. *Video Games*. Ann Arbor, MI: Cherry Lake Publishing, 2021.

Powell, Marie. *Asking Questions About Video Games*. Ann Arbor, MI: Cherry Lake Publishing, 2016.

## WEBSITES

### *Animal Crossing* Wiki
*https://animalcrossing.fandom.com/wiki/Animal_Crossing: _New_Horizons*
This fan-created site is packed with info about every detail of the *Animal Crossing* games.

### Island News — *Animal Crossing: New Horizons*
*https://www.animal-crossing.com/new-horizons/news*
Keep up to date with the latest official news updates about *Animal Crossing*.

# Index

## About the Author

Josh Gregory is the author of more than 150 books for kids. He has written about everything from animals to technology to history. A graduate of the University of Missouri–Columbia, he currently lives in Chicago, Illinois.